Hello, I'm Squiddy!

I was born in 2018. I belong to an artist called Squidoodle. You might have heard of him, but then again, maybe you haven't. He's a bit of a weirdo. I'm here to guide you through this book. You WILL get messy. You WILL get creative. You WILL have fun. I don't care if you're three years old or three hundred years old. The point of this book is to have fun, make things, play games, break the rules and unleash your inner artist.

You're gonna need glue, pens, pencils, crayons, markers, scissors, food, leaves, glitter, paint, stickers, in fact anything you can lay your mucky hands on.

Have fun!

FINISH THIS DOODLE-CITY

make sure you fill the whole page with castles and houses!

Be careful!

HOLD AN ICE CUBE UNTIL IT MELTS

SAY THE ALPHABET BACKWARDS

LICK YOUR OWN ELBOW

ACT LIKE A MONKEY

PEEL A BANANA USING ONLY YOUR THUMBS

STAND ON ONE FOOT FOR 2 MINUTES

THE DARE-DICE

Play with as many people as possible

Youngest person goes first

10 points for every dare completed

First to a hundred points wins!

Draw a selfie

(with a hat on)

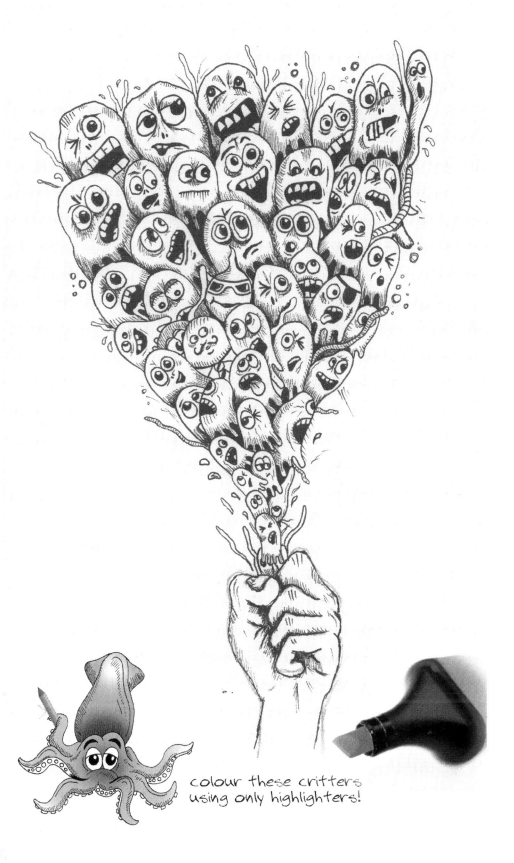

colour these critters
using only highlighters!

Color and cut out these horse saddles!

(you'll find out why on the next page)

cover this whole page
in leaves using
sticky tape

CAREFULLY CUT OUT SECTIONS 1, 2, 3, 4 AND 5 THEN
STICK A PHOTO OF YOURSELF ON THE OTHER SIDE FACING
IN.... YOU'RE IN JAIL!

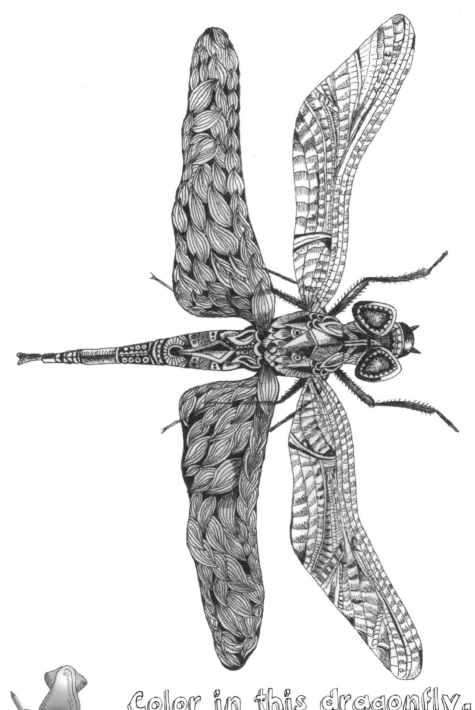

Color in this dragonfly, cut it out and stick it on your toilet seat!

WRITE A POEM IN WHITE
(CHALK OR PEN OR ANYTHING ELSE
YOU CAN FIND!!)

The Scroll of Honour

All the kids named below have helped out with ideas for the No-Rules Journal. If you see your name below, chances are your idea is in this book! If so, THANK YOU!!!!!

you're the best!

The Scroll of Honour

Shane Eadie

Sammy Allen

Christopher Allen

Eli Sutcliffe

Emma Hickson   Noah Husk

Raylan (Nat's kid)

Finn Hansen-McNamara

Lily Richardson

Noah Richardson

Alena Gonzalez

Amber Markley   Stevie Skelton

Adalaide Anderson

Ember Whawell

Sam Peach   Max Eadie

Pour a drip of your favourite

drink inside this circle

Stick a cool article from a magazine or catalogue in this space!

Color this palace using only one colored pencil

Having fun?

Good! Tear out this page and leave it under the doormat!

Make a paper
aeroplane out of this
page and launch it
from your bedroom
window!

...then step on it. (thanks Max!)

You know who would wear a suit like this? A parrot, Draw his head,

How to draw: A ZOMBIE!!!

Draw yours on the next page!

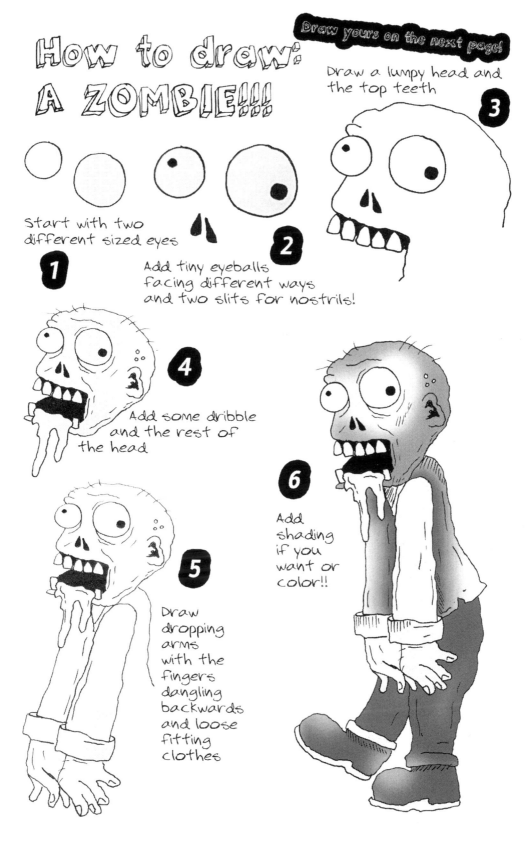

Draw a lumpy head and the top teeth

3

Start with two different sized eyes

1

Add tiny eyeballs facing different ways and two slits for nostrils!

2

4

Add some dribble and the rest of the head

6

Add shading if you want or color!!

5

Draw dropping arms with the fingers dangling backwards and loose fitting clothes

Cut out these leaves and stick them throughout the book

Spot the squiddy! There are 3 of me in this doodle but can you find them?

Write a list of things you should NEVER take in the bathtub with you!

I bet you can't name an animal using every letter of the alphabet......

a
b
c
d
e
f
g
h
i
j
k
l
m
n
o

p
q
r
s
t
u
v
w
x
y
z

not so subtle hint.....
this is a Quokka!!
(yeah I've never heard of them either!)

"Alpaca bag..." "No prob-llama."

Cut out this silly picture and give it to someone who might need cheering up.

grab your pens and color!

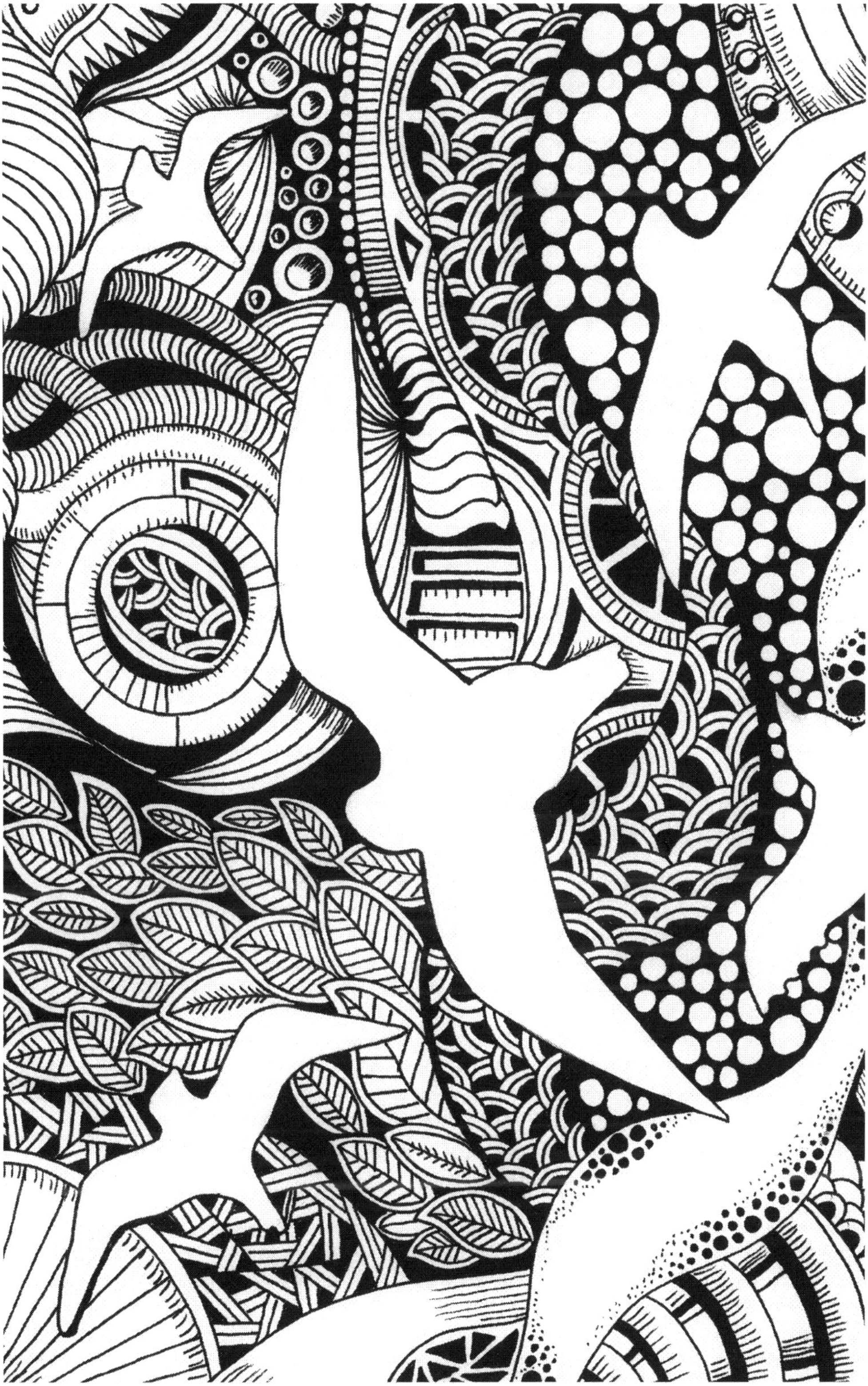

Fill one butterfly with scribbles and one with dots

Rip out this

page and put it in

your fridge overnight

grab your pens and color!

Find an old christmas or birthday card and stick it on this page

Make a list of your ideal gifts for Christmas or birthday

(I've helped you out with the first bit)

1   Every book by Steve Squidoodle Turner

OMG! Black snowflakes!

Surely you wouldn't want to cut them out and sprinkle them on someone's head would you?

MAKE YOUR OWN FORTUNE COOKIE THINGS

Cut out these fortunes and do something with them

You will probably eat a sausage at some point.

Someome will buy you some underwear.

This book tastes of chicken. Not really, it tastes of paper.

Meh.

This makes no sense.

Your lucky number is 765827345623649824673468273 6423

If you shake your hand above your head, nothing will happen.

You didn't actually eat this book did you?

You will find out that you have a hidden talent.
But then it will no longer be hidden.

Many a mickle makes a muckle.

Doodle this stag with patterns....

SCROLLS

Write your friend's names on these scrolls

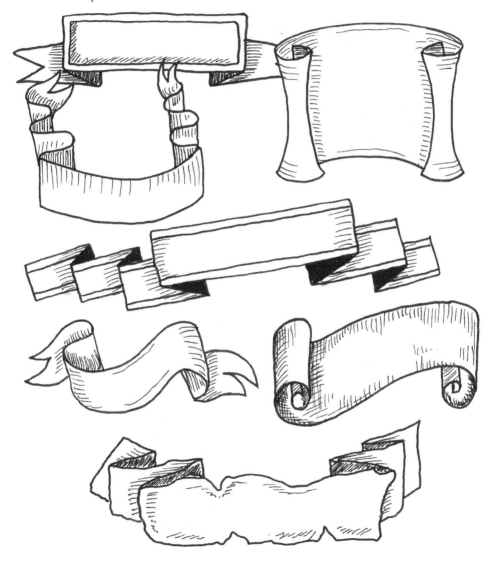

Color and cut out these feathers
.... leave a brightly coloured feather on
someone's pillow

Enjoying this book?

Don't forget to have a look at my website for loads more downloadable things!

www.squidoodleshop.com

Are your hands dirty?

EXCELLENT,
Make this page dirty as well.

Remove this page and roll it
tightly into a straw for
your next drink,
(plastic is bad for the ocean)

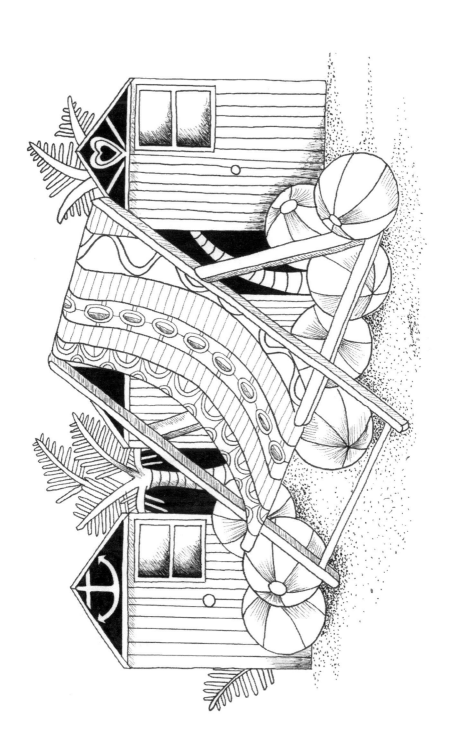

Color the B in yellow and black

Take this page with you to dinner - drip some of your dinner on the plate...

Remove this page and keep it in your pocket for three days

Fill the sea with doodles of fish!

grab your pens and color!

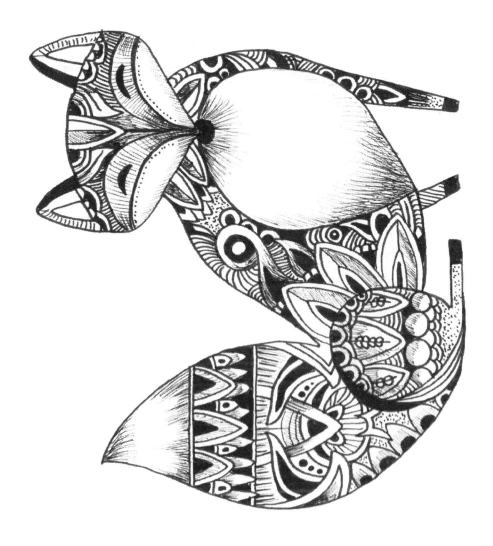

Make a list of all the cool places you've visited so far this year.

- - - - - - - - - - - - - - - - - - - -
- - - - - - - - - - - - - - - - - - - -
- - - - - - - - - - - - - - - - - - - -
- - - - - - - - - - - - - - - - - - - -
- - - - - - - - - - - - - - - - - - - -
- - - - - - - - - - - - - - - - - - - -
- - - - - - - - - - - - - - - - - - - -
- - - - - - - - - - - - - - - - - - - -
- - - - - - - - - - - - - - - - - - - -
- - - - - - - - - - - - - - - - - - - -
- - - - - - - - - - - - - - - - - - - -
- - - - - - - - - - - - - - - - - - - -
- - - - - - - - - - - - - - - - - - - -
- - - - - - - - - - - - - - - - - - - -

Sleep with the book under your pillow then write down your dream below...

Find a twig or a stick and figure out a way of attaching it to this page.

Cut out Squiddy and stick him
on top of the barcode
on the back of this book

grab your pens and color!

Cut out numbers from magazines
and newspapers and stick
them on this page.
(bet you can't get to 100)

Decorate the edges of the pages with colored pens whilst the book is closed!!

this bit!

Carefully cover this castle with glue using a glue stick, Then sprinkle sand on it!!

Stick one of the below things in this frame:
1. A band aid or plaster
2. A piece of food,
3. A stamp,
4. Your toenail clippings (ewww)

Cut out this square and use it to make a pocket. Stick the pocket on the inside of the front cover. Only stick the sides and the bottom so the top is free from glue. Then keep interesting things in it.

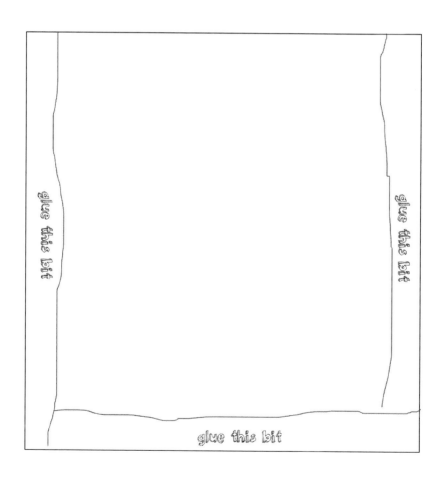

glue this bit

glue this bit

glue this bit

Keep coloring this circle using marker pens until the paper tears and it goes through to the next page......

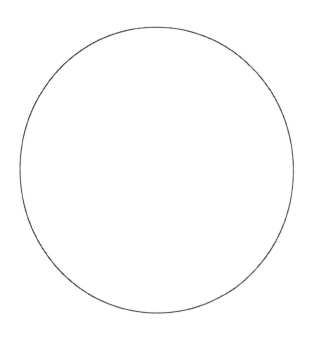

Stick a coin to this page then
leave the page somewhere for
a stranger to find it,
(if you're the stranger who has
found it, it is a random act
of kindness from someone pretty
awesome)

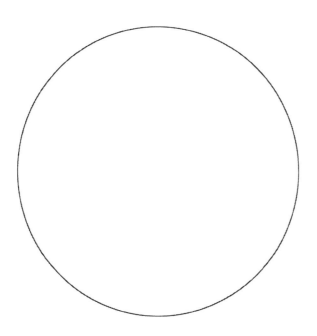

Remove this page,

Bury it in your garden,

Dig it up,

Stick it back in,

Take the book to school, college or wherever you work and get loads of people to sign this page.

Drip water on this page and let it dry crinkled

Draw round your foot
or hand and color it
in using something other
than pens or pencils

The Backwards Crossword

All the answers below need to be written backwards!! (Thanks Eli)

CLUES

Across

2. Small feline animal.
4. Things you wear on your feet.

Down

1. Dangerous animal in the sea.
3. The King of the jungle.

Color this car using an old toothbrush

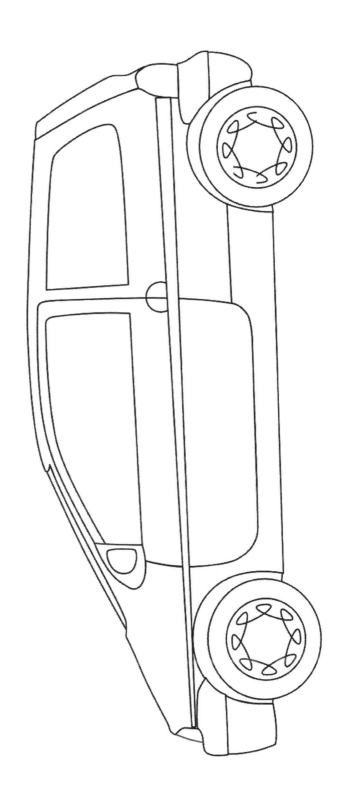

Can you read this page? No? Figure out a way to read it then. You might need to hold it up against something. Figured it out yet? You have? Well done you clever little monkey.

This is Englewither Flingle-slip.

Write a short story below about Englewither Flingle-slip and that one time he visited his friend Norbert the turtle but it rained all day and they both lost their pants down a drain.

Draw some silly legs on this spider,

Squiddy's Comic!

Draw your own comic strip about Squiddy!

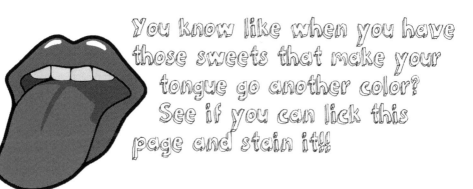

You know like when you have those sweets that make your tongue go another color? See if you can lick this page and stain it!!

We're nearly at the end of the book.
Does it look all battered and used and
stuff? AWESOME!!!!
Now close the book tightly, jump on
it three times, slide it across the room,
ride over it on your bike, place it under
a chair leg or bite it. Your choice.

Remove this page and freeze it in an ice cube tray

100 bonus points if you can thaw it out and stick it back in.

Draw some silly
creatures in the corners
then fold them over

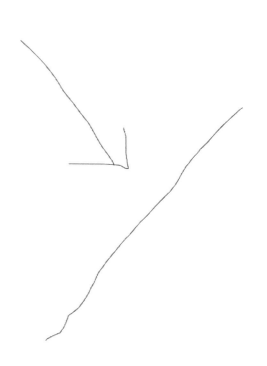

Take a photo of your hand holding the book up somewhere interesting.

Make sure you send the photo to my art page on facebook (or get someone to do it for you) and I'll share it in a special album!

www.facebook.com/SquidDoodleArt

When I've got loads I'll pick one lucky winner who'll get some signed artwork and other books!

Flick back through all the tasks you've done.
Which was your favourite?
Draw a picture of you completing your
favourite page below!

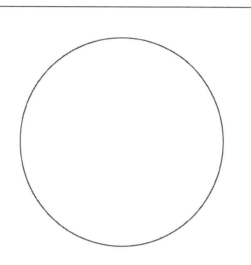

DO NOT DISTURB!
I'm working on
the
No Rules Journal

Hold a pen in your mouth and write your name below.

My name is _____

This was my attempt.....

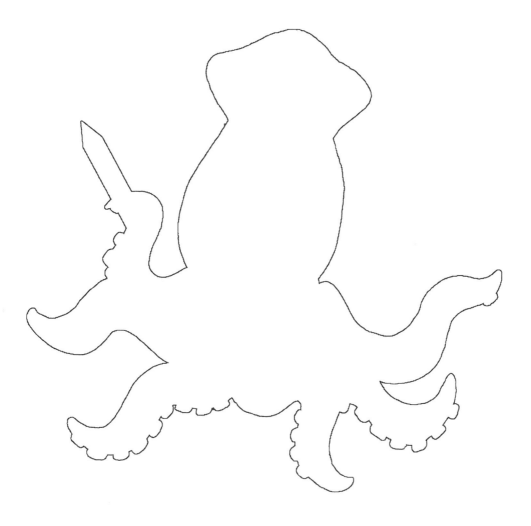

DRAW YOUR OWN SQUIDDY!

I've done an outline
to start you off.

You've finished the book!
...have a medal

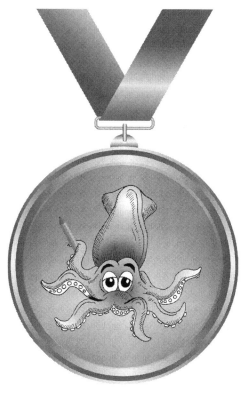

One last thing to do....
Grab your book, run to
the top of the stairs and yell

I DID IT!!

I hope you enjoyed the book. You can find loads
more downloads on my website
www.squidoodleshop.com
Don't forget to check out my facebook and instagram pages
to find out when I will release another book.

www.facebook.com/SquidDoodleArt
www.instagram.com/squidoodleart

Made in the USA
San Bernardino, CA
26 January 2020